Our Endangered Planet
POPULATION GROWTH

Suzanne Winckler
and
Mary M. Rodgers

LERNER PUBLICATIONS COMPANY • MINNEAPOLIS

Thanks to Sharyn Fenwick, James E. Laib, Kerstin Coyle, Zachary Marell, and Gary Hansen for their help in preparing this book.

Words that appear in **bold** type are listed in a glossary that starts on page 60.

LIBRARY OF CONGRESS CATALOGING-IN-PUBLICATION DATA

Winckler, Suzanne, 1946–
   Our endangered planet. Population growth / Suzanne Winckler and Mary M. Rodgers.
     p.   cm.
   Includes bibliographical references and index.
   Summary: Studies the effects of uncontrolled population growth on the global environment, which results in dangerous pressures on natural resources, wildlife, air, water, and living space.
   ISBN 0-8225-2502-X (lib. bdg.)
   1. Population—Juvenile literature. 2. Population policy—Juvenile literature. 3. Human ecology—Juvenile literature. 4. Environmental policy—Juvenile literature. [1. Population. 2. Environmental policy.] I. Rodgers, Mary M. (Mary Madeline), 1954–   . II. Title. III. Series: Our endangered planet (Minneapolis, Minn.)
HB883.W56   1990
304.6'2—dc20   90–41996
                              CIP
                              AC

Manufactured in the United States of America

2 3 4 5 6 7 8 9 10 00 99 98 97 96 95 94 93 92 91

Front cover: The growth of the earth's population becomes clear in sprawling urban areas, where people and cars vie for space. Back cover: (Left) Egypt, a large country in northern Africa, has a rapidly expanding population. As a result, crowded streets are common in Egyptian cities. (Right) Rich nations have low rates of population growth but use much more of the earth's natural resources, such as petroleum.

Recycled paper

All paper used in this book is of recycled material and may be recycled.

Recyclable

CONTENTS

OUR ENDANGERED PLANET

In the 1960s, astronauts first traveled beyond the earth's protective atmosphere and were able to look back at our planet. What they saw was a beautiful globe, turning slowly in space. That image reminds us that our home planet has limits, for we know of no other place that can support life.

The various parts of our natural environment—including air, water, soil, plants, and animals—are partners in making our planet a good place to live. If we endanger one element, the other partners are badly affected, too.

People throughout the world are working to protect and heal the earth's environment. They recognize that making nature our ally and not our victim is the way to shape a common future. Because we have only one planet to share, its health and survival mean that we all can live.

In 1991, the number of human beings on our planet increased by about 87 million. This increase was larger than any other year's population growth in history. About 90 percent of this growth happened in the world's poorest countries. These nations already have a hard time providing food, education, and jobs for their citizens.

But population growth means more than just greater numbers of people. This issue also involves how people use and take care of resources—things like water, fuel, and air.

Although poorer countries bring more children into the world, richer countries use far more resources. Both activities damage the health of our planet. The more we learn about how our behavior affects the earth, the wiser we can be in making choices that preserve our home for future generations.

CHAPTER ONE

My, How We've Grown

Our planet is filling up with people. In 1991, the world's population was 5.3 billion. It is expected to double to 10 billion by the year 2027.

Each day, about 400,000 babies are born on our planet. On the same day, about 140,000 people die. If we subtract the deaths from the births, we come up with the number 260,000.

This means that, before you go to bed tonight, there will be 260,000 more people in the world than there were yesterday. That is roughly how many people live in the city of Tallahassee, Florida; of Asmara, Ethiopia; or of Valparaiso, Chile.

Many people worry that the earth will not be able to provide enough food, water, and space for everyone in the years to come. They are also concerned about educating all these newcomers and supplying them with jobs and good health care. Think of the places you visit every week. Look at your classroom, the streets in your

(Left) **These triplets are from Cameroon, a fast-growing country in central Africa.** *(Above)* **Students of all ages share the reading materials at a school in Saudi Arabia.**

neighborhood, and the grocery store where your parents shop. Can these spaces hold twice as many people?

THE FAST TRACK

Figuring out how fast our population is growing is not a simple matter of addition and subtraction. We determine the **population growth rate** by comparing the rate, or speed, at which people are born to the rate at which they die.

When births and deaths are about equal, the population is stable, meaning it is not increasing at all. This situation is known as **zero population growth (ZPG).** The people who support ZPG recommend that each family produce two children or fewer to keep the world's population from growing. Stable growth, they believe, would help all people live better lives. ZPG also lessens the demand on our planet's natural resources, such as water, fuel, and air.

But for many years now, the **birth rate** has outpaced the **death rate,** meaning more people are being born than are dying. The world's annual population growth rate is about 1.7 percent. That figure appears to be a very small increase from 0 per-

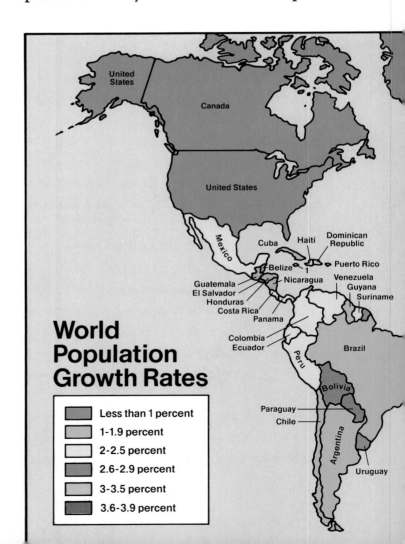

World Population Growth Rates

▨	Less than 1 percent
▨	1-1.9 percent
▨	2-2.5 percent
▨	2.6-2.9 percent
▨	3-3.5 percent
▨	3.6-3.9 percent

cent, or ZPG. Why are people concerned about what seems to be a small number?

When the birth rate is even slightly higher than the death rate, more children grow up to become adults. These adults, in turn, have more children. Within the next 25 years, roughly three billion young people will become old enough to have

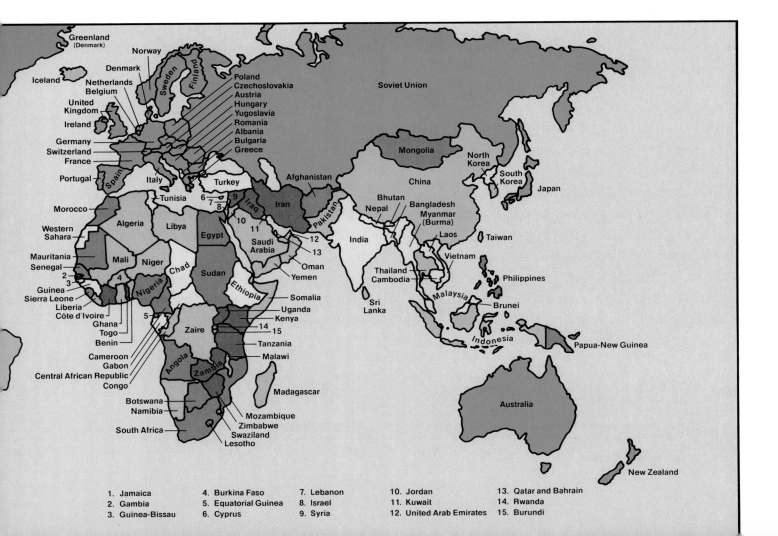

1. Jamaica	4. Burkina Faso	7. Lebanon	10. Jordan	13. Qatar and Bahrain
2. Gambia	5. Equatorial Guinea	8. Israel	11. Kuwait	14. Rwanda
3. Guinea-Bissau	6. Cyprus	9. Syria	12. United Arab Emirates	15. Burundi

babies. *The bigger the population, the faster it grows.* Populations increase by multiplication, not addition. This is the difference between $2 \times 2 \times 2 \times 2$ and $2 + 2 + 2 + 2$.

Ten thousand years ago, the earth held about five million people. This number equals the current population of Philadelphia, Pennsylvania, or of Guangzhou (Canton), China. It took 8,000 years for the world's population to reach 130 million. In another 1,840 years, the population reached one billion.

In about 1840, however, the number of people on our planet began to grow very quickly. Within only 100 years, the world's population increased from 1 billion to 2.5 billion. Within another 50 years, it went up from 2.5 billion to 5 billion! We will reach the 6 billion mark by the year 2000, and by 2027, our planet is expected to be home to 10 billion people.

CHANGING TIMES

Why has the world's population grown so fast in the last 150 years? Beginning in the 1800s, many aspects of human life changed. Farms grew in size and number. New farming methods and better seeds increased annual harvests. People had more food to eat, and countries began buying and selling goods throughout the world. With the invention of new machines, people moved these goods—and themselves—quickly, first in steamships, then in trains, cars, and airplanes.

After farming methods and transportation improved, cheap food became available to more people. Before these discoveries,

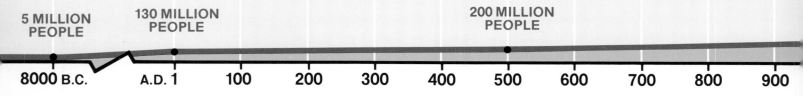

5 MILLION PEOPLE

130 MILLION PEOPLE

200 MILLION PEOPLE

8000 B.C.   A.D. 1   100   200   300   400   500   600   700   800   900

famines—severe shortages of food—regularly caused widespread starvation. Famine is now a rare event in most parts of the world.

MEDICAL MARVELS

In addition to inventing ways to grow more food, scientists also discovered what caused some deadly diseases and infections. These scientists found out that certain **bacteria** (very tiny organisms) make us sick when they enter and grow in our bodies. After the invention of the microscope, scientists could see these tiny life forms and could learn how they caused sickness.

This important breakthrough helped to stop the spread of illnesses that pass rapidly from person to person through a population. These widespread diseases, known as

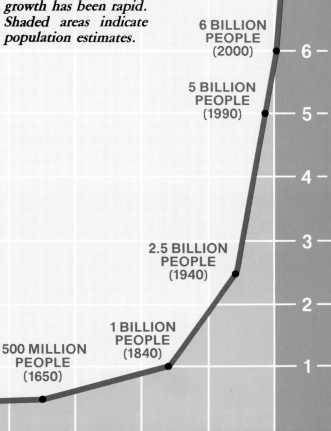

This chart shows how our numbers have increased. The earth's population rose very slowly for thousands of years. Since about 1840, however, growth has been rapid. Shaded areas indicate population estimates.

10 BILLION PEOPLE (2027)

6 BILLION PEOPLE (2000)

5 BILLION PEOPLE (1990)

2.5 BILLION PEOPLE (1940)

1 BILLION PEOPLE (1840)

500 MILLION PEOPLE (1650)

275 MILLION PEOPLE

Billions of People

10 9 8 7 6 5 4 3 2 1

1000 1100 1200 1300 1400 1500 1600 1700 1800 1900 2000

epidemics, included malaria, **influenza,** and yellow fever.

An epidemic can strike people of all ages and can cause sudden declines in population. The last worldwide epidemic—in this case, of influenza—occurred between 1918 and 1919. In those years, the flu killed roughly 20 million people around the world. In New York City alone, 12,500

A traveling nurse in Chile—a long, narrow nation in South America—gives shots to a rural family. The medicines prevent people from getting some common diseases.

people, out of a population of about 3 million, died of influenza.

To halt the spread of such diseases, we began to control harmful bacteria where they lived. For example, we developed a way to eliminate them from our drinking water. In addition, scientists invented medicines called **antibiotics** that help a person's body to fight diseases caused by bacteria.

Scientists also discovered a method, called **immunization,** to control diseases. After getting a tiny dose of a particular bacterium, the human body then develops immunity (resistance) to the disease the bacterium causes. Doctors can now immunize people against smallpox, typhoid, and polio, for example.

LIVING LONGER

The revolutions in farming, transportation, and medicine have greatly boosted world population. In the United States, for instance, **infant mortality** (the number of newborns that die as infants) has sharply declined. In 1915, 100 U.S. babies out of 1,000 died as infants. By 1991, the number had dropped to about 9 out of 1,000.

Life expectancy, or how long a person is likely to live, depends on factors such as health care and how much food is available. In 1900, the life expectancy of a white male in the United States was 46.6

These students in Hokkaido, Japan, benefit from a good education. The Japanese also have strong health-care services, which contribute to the country's high life expectancy figure of 79 years.

In Afghanistan, the life expectancy of the people is very low—only 41 years—because of war and disease.

years. By 1990, a white U.S. male could plan on living to be about 72 years old.

Other parts of the world tell different stories. In Afghanistan, a war-torn country in southern Asia, the infant mortality rate in 1991 was 182 deaths in every 1,000 live births. In Japan, a wealthy Asian nation, the number was 5 per 1,000. In Afghanistan, average life expectancy in 1991 was 41, while in Japan it was 79.

CHAPTER TWO

DIFFERENT STROKES FOR DIFFERENT FOLKS

If you visited Ticul, a village in southern Mexico, or Nairobi, a big city in the African country of Kenya, you would notice that our planet is home to many different cultures and styles of living. People around the world do not look alike, eat the same food, dress alike, or listen to similar music.

There are also great differences around the world in the **standard of living—** the measure of how safely and comfortably people live. People do not have equal chances to make money. Nor do they have the same opportunities to buy the things

(Left) Girls in Côte d'Ivoire, a West African nation once called Ivory Coast, wear shells and headdresses to participate in a religious ceremony. (Right) A teacher in Australia explains the rules of a relay race to three young runners.

15

that money provides, such as food, housing, education, and health care.

Some people always have lots of food, while others go hungry. Some people can buy anything they want, while others have to stand in line to purchase a loaf of bread.

This Ethiopian boy is among the one billion people on our planet who do not have enough to eat.

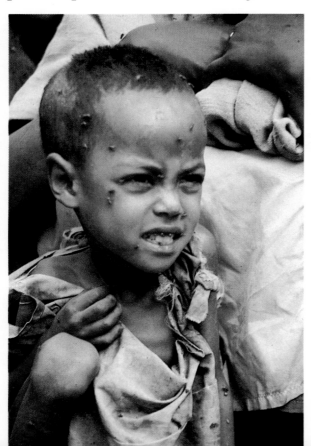

THE GLOBAL TEETER-TOTTER

Of the five billion people on earth, a little more than one billion have a high standard of living. These families have plenty to eat, live in comfortable houses, and usually own at least one car. The children go to school, and the adults have jobs.

The other four billion have a lower standard of living. They have less to eat. They may lack a good education or a well-paying job. They probably do not own a car or a television.

Of these four billion people, *one billion* live in severe poverty. They are hungry or sick or both. Most of them are not educated. They do not have jobs or are too ill to work.

A family's standard of living, in part, depends on where the family lives. Economists—people who study how nations and people manage their money—classify the world's countries into two groups.

The **developed nations** have created wealth from the earth's natural resources, such as forests, farmland, seas, and mineral deposits. To process these resources, the developed nations have built industries, which employ most of their people. Thus, developed countries are also often called **industrialized nations.**

The developed nations educate their citizens, support hospitals, and build roads. Developed nations are rich, and most of their citizens have a high standard of living. The United States, Canada, Sweden, Switzerland, Australia, and Japan are examples of developed nations.

Economists have called the second group **developing nations** or **Third-World countries.** The names mean that these countries are developing their natural resources but are not as industrialized as the developed nations are. Third-World countries are less likely to have enough jobs, housing, and health care for their people. Among the developing nations are Brazil, Egypt, Kenya, Pakistan, and Indonesia.

Demographers (people who study population traits) point out that the populations of Third-World countries are increasing much faster than the populations of the developed nations. The average yearly rate of

Using modern machinery, developed nations can grow the food that their citizens need.

population growth in developed countries is less than 1 (.5) percent. The average rate for Third-World countries is much higher—2.1 percent.

These figures are calculated after the death rate is subtracted from the birth rate. The leftover births show us how fast a population is increasing. For example, out of a sample of 1,000 members of a developed nation's population, 5 *more* people are added each year. In the Third World, out of 1,000 people, 21 additional people are counted.

Many Third-World countries are growing even faster than the average. For example, the growth rates of Kenya and Zambia in Africa and of Jordan and Syria in the Middle East are each about 4 percent —the highest rate in the world. Demographers estimate that Kenya's population of 25 million will more than double to 60 million in the next 30 years!

This chart finds the rate of population growth for a make-believe country of 1,000 people. In the top equations, we subtract deaths from births to arrive at the number of new people and then add the newcomers to the total population. In the bottom equation, we divide the total new population (1,021) by the old population (1,000). We then multiply the result (1.021) by 100 to make a percent (102.1%). By subtracting 100, we remove 100 percent of the old population. The result (2.1%) gives us the growth rate caused by new people.

$$\begin{array}{ll} 31 \text{ births} & 1{,}000 \ (\text{old population}) \\ \underline{-10 \text{ deaths}} & \underline{+ \ 21 \ (\text{new people})} \\ 21 \text{ new people} & 1{,}021 \ (\text{new population}) \end{array}$$

$$\frac{1{,}021}{1{,}000} = 1.021 \times 100\% = 102.1\% - 100\% = 2.1\%$$

POPULATION PUZZLE

Hundreds of years ago, day-to-day survival depended on help from every member of the family. Even young children had to work to supply food or money. Parents expected their grown children to take care of them in their old age. Infant mortality was usually very high. Women had many babies to increase the chances that at least some children would survive to become adults.

In countries with a high standard of living, these family patterns have changed. For example, babies born in developed nations are very likely to grow up strong and healthy. Most children no longer work in the fields or in factories. Instead, they go to school.

When children are older, they often move away from their parents. Fewer adult children care for their aging parents. Instead, more elderly people live in retirement homes and health-care centers. Many women in industrialized countries now work away from the home and have less time to raise large families.

In Third-World countries, however, these changes in family life have not occurred. Families still have a strong desire to have many children for the same reasons that existed hundreds of years ago.

At the same time, immunization and better health care have reduced death rates in these developing nations. Thus, in the Third World, death rates have declined, but birth rates remain high. This situation has created a serious population problem.

To have zero population growth, or ZPG, in the developing countries, one of these rates must be altered. A catastrophe —like a shortage of food—might trigger famine, which would cause the death rate to rise. But no one wants such a tragic event to happen. A better way to achieve stable population growth is to reduce the number of births per family—that is, to lower the birth rate.

HOW MUCH DO WE COST?

A rapidly expanding population can be hard for a nation to handle. For example, local farmers may have difficulty growing enough food for everyone. Bringing in food from another part of the world may be expensive. If the population grows too fast, jobs may be scarce and schools may become overcrowded.

But overpopulation is costly not only to Third-World countries. In developed nations, such as the United States, people have become used to a high standard of living. In maintaining this lifestyle, they use a huge share of the world's food, minerals, and energy. These countries also pollute air, water, and soil more than Third-World nations do.

For example, although the United States holds 5 percent of the world's population, it uses 28 percent of the world's energy. Over time, a U.S. baby will consume far more of the world's resources than a baby who is born in an underdeveloped country.

Thus, population growth is an issue with two parts. The first involves *numbers,* and the second concerns *use of resources.* These two parts give all of us a role in solving the world's population problems.

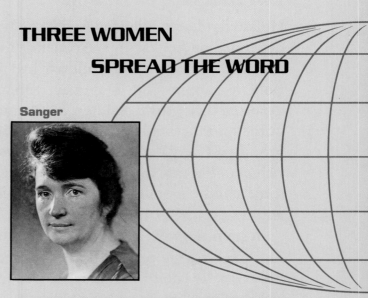

THREE WOMEN SPREAD THE WORD

Sanger

During the twentieth century, three women became pioneers in the struggle to limit births and to reduce our use of the earth's resources. The sixth of eleven children, Margaret Sanger was born in New York in 1883. Sanger believed that every woman should be allowed to plan the size of her family. After becoming a nurse, Sanger worked in the poorest sections of New York City. She saw many deaths among infants and mothers, some of whom died in childbirth. Sanger also treated women who were sick from having too many babies.

Brundtland

Stopes

In the early 1900s, it was illegal in the United States to supply information about birth control. Through her writings and lectures, Sanger tried to educate women about limiting the sizes of their families. For this work, she was arrested in 1914 but was quickly released. In 1916, she opened the first U.S. birth-control clinic. Because this action broke the law, Sanger served 30 days in jail. The clinic stayed open, however, and the police raided it in 1929.

These events drew attention to Sanger's work. Slowly, people began to agree with her goals. By 1936, it was no longer a crime to supply information about birth control.

While Sanger worked in the United States, Marie Stopes led the birth-control movement in Great Britain. She founded her country's first birth-control clinic in 1921 and wrote about the history and practice of birth control.

Stopes was writing when any discussion of how to limit family size was unpopular. Her books sparked opposition from religious groups. In time, however, some churches changed their views on birth control.

In the 1980s, Gro Harlem Brundtland chaired the United Nations World Commission on Environment and Development. At the same time, she served twice as the prime minister of Norway. Before getting into politics, Brundtland earned her degree as a medical doctor while raising four children with her husband.

Speaking often about worldwide environmental issues, Brundtland thinks that all people must work together to protect our planet. She also believes that citizens of the developed world use too many natural resources. By talking about the impact of our actions, Brundtland hopes we will take better care of the earth.

CHAPTER THREE

THE HOUSE WE LIVE IN

The earth is a complex **ecosystem,** or place where living and nonliving things interact with each other in many different ways. Humans are one **species,** or kind, of living thing. Besides ourselves, living things include all types of animals and plants—everything from whales to shamrocks. Estimates of how many different species live on our planet range from 5 million to 30 million!

The nonliving things in our ecosystem include the air and water that all species need for survival and the soil that grows plants. **Fossil fuels**—such as petroleum and coal—are also part of the nonliving ecosystem. We use fossil fuels to run cars and to operate factories.

Our ecosystem has not always been the way it is today. Our planet is billions of years old, and it has changed in that

(Left) **The plants and animals in this tropical rain forest in southeastern Asia work together as a balanced, natural unit.** *(Above)* **Fossil fuels, such as petroleum, are also part of our natural world and are made into gasoline at large refineries.**

time. Until recently, natural events—a long period of unbearably cold weather, for example—caused the most important changes. But for about the last 200 years, humans and their activities have been the major agents of change. Because there are so many of us, our actions make a big difference in the earth's ecosystem.

SHARING EARTH'S HOUSE

Most of us think of our planet as a vast place. The earth has limits, however, and

Lifting an earthenware container, a young man from Central America takes a welcome swallow of water—one of our planet's limited resources.

can supply only so much food, absorb only so much garbage, and produce only so much clean air.

Many of the earth's natural resources are **finite,** or limited. There is, for instance, a finite amount of water on earth. Every person requires water for survival and cleanliness. Without water to drink, we would die. In developed countries, water is used in many ways. It creates energy in dams, cools off machinery in factories, and irrigates farmland.

Some finite resources, such as water and air, are reusable. Others are **exhaustible,** meaning that once we have used up these resources, they will be gone forever. For example, it took millions of years for fossil fuels to form within the earth. But we are burning these fuels so quickly that they may be exhausted within the next century.

One way to understand the relationship between population and resources is by thinking of the earth as your house. Imagine what would happen if your next-door neighbors moved in with your family tomorrow. The arrival of these newcomers—

who did not bring any food, furniture, money, or clothing—would change life at your home.

You would have to share your bedroom, clothes, books, and bike. There would be more people to feed, so everyone would have to eat less. Your parents might have to work longer to make more money to buy additional food. The household would need more water for drinking, bathing, and cooking. If we enlarge this situation, we can see what could happen to the earth if the population doubles by 2027.

EARLY WARNINGS

People have long talked about the "ideal" size of the human population. In 1798, for instance, the British economist Thomas Malthus compared human populations and food production. He noted that our numbers increase faster than the rate at which we can grow food. Since food is necessary for survival, Malthus believed that food shortages would be the main factor limiting population growth.

Thomas Malthus studied how large populations and low food supplies affect each other.

Malthus did not predict the introduction of **fertilizers** (chemicals that help plants grow), better seeds, and more efficient farming techniques. These improvements boosted food production around the world in the nineteenth and twentieth centuries. Modern farming methods have allowed us to feed ourselves much better than Malthus had imagined. As a result, his theory fell out of fashion.

However, one billion people—one-fifth of the earth's entire population—go hungry every day. Modern farming practices put pressure on the earth's ecosystem. For example, **pesticides** (chemicals that kill insects) and fertilizers are poisoning our water and soil. Overcutting of forests and

As it flows through Africa, the Nile River picks up rich topsoil that makes the waterway look reddish brown in color.

Planes spray pesticides to kill insects that destroy crops. This practice has helped us to grow more food. The chemicals in the pesticides also poison water and soil and become stored in the bodies of animals.

of other vegetation takes away roots that hold **topsoil** (the surface soil in which plants grow). Rainfall and floods then wash away this rich soil. In our search for more irrigation water, we are also exhausting aquifers (underground water supplies).

Another warning came from the Swedish scientist Svante August Arrhenius in

Factories often use coal to run their machinery. When burned, this mineral sends carbon dioxide (CO_2) into the air.

the 1880s. He noticed that, since the early 1700s—when the number of factories began to rise—humans have been burning coal at a fast rate. As it burns, coal releases **carbon dioxide (CO_2)** into the air. In certain amounts, this odorless and colorless gas is a natural part of our atmosphere. But cars and factories put more and more CO_2 into the air every year, and the gas traps the earth's heat.

Arrhenius predicted that increased amounts of CO_2 would raise the earth's temperature. Warmer temperatures, in turn, would melt ice caps and would add more water to the seas. As a result of a warmer climate, rainfall levels could decrease and crops could fail. Although other scientists valued Arrhenius's research, the general public has largely ignored his findings until lately.

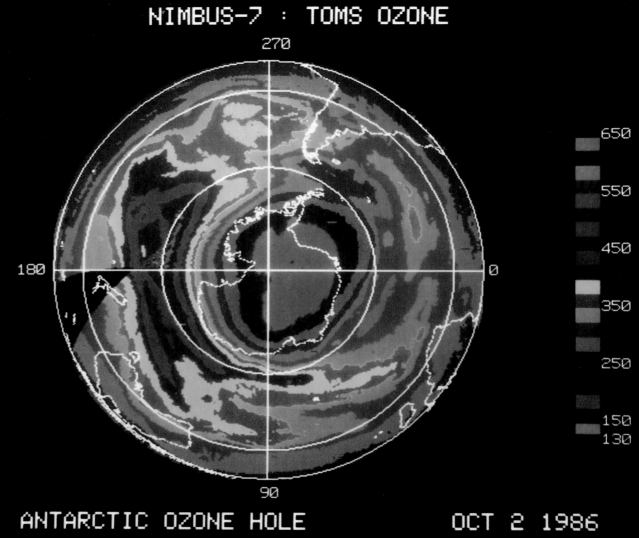

CHAPTER FOUR

SIGNS OF GLOBAL STRESS

In the past, changes in the earth's ecosystem usually happened over a longer period than one human lifetime. People adjusted fairly easily to the small changes that did occur. More recently, scientists have begun to tell us that the earth's ecosystem is showing signs of stress. The rapid increase in the human population is one strain, and it worsens the other stresses. Let's look at additional problems confronting our planet.

BATTERING OUR SHIELD

Ozone is a gas made of oxygen atoms. It forms a fragile, natural shield high above

(Left) The purple splotch on this computer map of Antarctica shows where our atmosphere's protective shield, called the ozone layer, is dangerously thin.

the earth's surface that filters out harmful rays from the sun. In 1974 two scientists in California discovered that chemicals called **chloro-fluoro-carbons (CFCs)** were drifting upward into the ozone layer.

At this height, the CFCs break apart, and parts of the compounds destroy the ozone. As a result of this chemical reaction, the shield is thinning. Scientists predict that if the ozone layer does not stop thinning, crops will fail more often, sea life will be damaged, and cases of skin cancer will increase.

People in developed countries rely heavily on CFCs. The chemicals are the coolants in air conditioners and refrigerators and are used as cleaning fluids in many industries. CFCs are needed to make plastic goods, including Styrofoam containers. CFCs are also propellants. They push the liquid out of spray cans, delivering a mist of paint or deodorant at the push of a button.

In 1990, more than 80 countries, including the United States, said they would ban the production and use of CFCs by the year 2000. But many other nations still allow CFCs to be used as propellants. Even with a worldwide ban, it would take more than 100 years for the CFCs already swirling around our planet to disappear.

WARMING UP TO ACID RAIN

As cars and factories give off more fumes, CO_2 continues to build up in the earth's atmosphere. The long-term effects of the buildup are hotly debated around the world. Many scientists now support the predictions that Arrhenius made more than 100 years ago. They warn that even a slight increase in the earth's temperature will affect many things in our lives.

For example, summers will be longer and hotter. Icy areas will melt, and rainfall will decline. Since rain is needed to nourish crops, growing food will become more difficult. Sea levels will rise, flooding coastal cities and low-lying islands.

Along with creating CO_2, burning fossil fuels in automobiles and factories produces

Some scientists think that if the earth's temperatures continue to increase, icy areas will melt and cause sea levels to rise. As a result, low-lying pieces of land, such as the Florida Keys, may be flooded.

Acid rain falls on forests throughout the world, eating away at healthy trees until they are too weak to survive.

sulfur and nitrogen oxides. These chemical compounds drift upward and combine with the water vapor that is part of our atmosphere. The oxides and water form acid solutions, which fall back to earth in rain. Around the world, this acid rain is destroying lakes, rivers, forests, and buildings.

GOING UP IN SMOKE

Throughout the **tropics**—the warm, rainy area around the earth's equator—people are cutting and burning forests to make pasture for cattle and fields for crops. The large-scale cutting and burning of forests, called **deforestation**, releases CO_2 into the atmosphere and contributes to global warming. In 1987, the fires from burning trees in Brazil were the source of about one-fifth of all the CO_2 released into the atmosphere in that year.

Deforestation causes other problems, such as **erosion** (the loss of valuable topsoil) and flooding. Trees and their root systems serve as giant sponges, capturing rainfall and slowing water flow. After trees have been cut down, water rushes over the land. In some cases, the water carries away the topsoil. In addition, the surging water floods the surrounding area, destroying

crops, homes, and businesses. In 1988, floods from deforestation in the southern Asian country of Bangladesh left about 25 million people homeless.

TIRING THE LAND

A desert is a dry, barren place. Humans sometimes create deserts by cutting down all the vegetation or by putting too many animals on the land to graze. The process is called **desertification,** or the making of deserts. Abused in this way, land that should be fruitful cannot produce food or support livestock.

But people often do not intend to create deserts. They are usually trying to find wood for fuel or to grow more food or to raise more livestock. All of these activities help them to care for their families. In many countries, desertification is a direct

Once covered with tropical rain forests, the Dominican Republic—a nation in the Caribbean Sea—has almost completely cleared these woodlands to make farmland.

In Morocco, North Africa, workers have planted palm and tamarisk trees to keep sand from the Sahara Desert away from valuable cropland.

result of families scratching a living from overworked or deforested land.

Desertification most often happens in places where human populations are rapidly expanding. The West African country of Mali, where the annual rate of population growth is 3 percent, has seen more land become desert in recent years. Other areas that are turning into deserts include parts of northern, eastern, and southern Africa, of south central Asia, and of southern South America.

LOSING OUR PARTNERS

We share the earth with billions of other living creatures. Humans have changed the earth's ecosystem to grow food, to build

Ashy dogweed may become extinct by 1995. Now found only in Texas, the plant has lost its habitat because of industrial and housing projects.

dams, and to expand cities. In achieving these goals, we have made parts of the planet unfit for many other species of plants and animals. We have also killed animals for food and sport and have poisoned other creatures with chemicals. When all the individual members of a species of plant or animal die, that species becomes **extinct.**

The peregrine falcon is an endangered bird of prey. Its numbers dropped dramatically in the 1970s, when the pesticide DDT became stored in the small birds that peregrines ate for food. As a result, DDT also got into the bodies of peregrines. The poison makes the shell of the bird's egg easy to break and too dry for the baby inside to survive. Ending the use of DDT worldwide would help the peregrine falcon to fight extinction.

The extinction of the passenger pigeon in North America shows humankind's ability to get rid of even common species. The passenger pigeon was probably the most abundant bird ever to live on earth. For many decades, people in the United States hunted passenger pigeons for food and for sport and used the birds' feathers to stuff pillows. By 1900, hunting had reduced the billions of passenger pigeons to only a handful. The world's last passenger pigeon died in a zoo in Cincinnati, Ohio, in 1914.

The extinction of living creatures is a natural process. Dinosaurs, for example, became extinct before humans ever lived on earth. The rate of extinction, however, has sped up since humans have inhabited the planet. Some of the creatures we have already lost include the elephant bird (extinct by about 1700), Stellar's sea cow (1768), and the zebra-like quagga (1883).

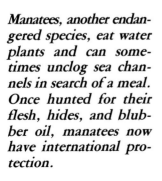

Manatees, another endangered species, eat water plants and can sometimes unclog sea channels in search of a meal. Once hunted for their flesh, hides, and blubber oil, manatees now have international protection.

CHAPTER FIVE

PACING OURSELVES

We have seen how 5 billion of us are changing the earth's ecosystem. Imagine what would happen if there were 10 billion people, the estimated population by the year 2027. If we want to live healthy lives, to protect the earth's ecosystem, and to save other species from extinction, we must all work together to manage human population growth.

RUNNING ON EMPTY

Scientists warn that if we do not slow our population growth, then the earth will control this growth for us, perhaps in ways we will not like. The earth's resources will be reduced or they will simply run out. This situation is like driving a car when the gas gauge hits the "empty" mark. Running on empty is a risky thing to do.

(Left) **A crowd of children in the Central African Republic wave from the field beside their school. *(Above)* As our population grows, it puts more pressure on our water resources, which we use for bathing, drinking, and cooking.**

As our planet's population grows larger, it will become harder to feed everyone. Famine could happen in some parts of the world. Developed and developing countries could fight over scarcer food. People weakened by hunger could catch all sorts of diseases. This picture of the future is bleak. It means great human sadness and suffering. A better solution is to control our growth.

But let's clear up one important misunderstanding. Some people mistakenly think that ZPG means having no children at all. Regulating population does not mean people cannot have families. It means instead that we need to make birth rates and death rates match. They are about equal when one new baby replaces each person who dies. If each family in the world had no more than two children and if the death rate remained stable, we would achieve ZPG.

FAMILY PLANS

For thousands of years, families have made plans. They plan when to plant gardens and when to harvest them. They decide when to go to bed at night and when to wake up in the morning. They discuss how much money to spend on food and other goods and how much money to save. These plans become part of the rhythm of family life. More and more families are now planning the number of children they will have. These plans vary around the world and among different cultures and classes of people.

Couples that have only two children help to achieve zero population growth.

CROWDED STREETS IN BRAZIL

The city of São Paulo [above] in Brazil has a population of about seven million. Many of its poorest residents live in favelas [left].

With more than 150 million people, Brazil is the largest country in size and population in South America. One-third of all Brazilians are younger than 15, and roughly one-twentieth are older than 65. About three-fourths of the people live in cities.

One of these urban dwellers is eleven-year-old Iris Mendes. The second of six children, she moved with her family to São Paulo in southeastern Brazil a few years ago. Jobs are scarce in this growing city. Many of the people live in slums called favelas. The members of the Mendes family struggle to feed, clothe, and shelter themselves. Iris used to go to school but now helps gather discarded vegetables to resell in her mother's food stall.

Until 1984, the government of Brazil did not have a family-planning program and believed rapid population growth was good. As the country's city populations increased, however, Brazil's officials realized that smaller families would make jobs, food, and education more easily available to people like Iris and her family. People can now obtain all forms of birth control in Brazil, and two-thirds of Brazil's married women limit the number of children they have.

The key to careful family planning is **contraception** or **birth control**—the use of a method, device, or drug that keeps a woman from having a baby. Many different kinds of birth control exist, and families have long used one form or another to prevent pregnancy.

Before the invention of modern contraceptives, people practiced birth control through age-old customs. These practices included **prolonged breastfeeding** (allowing a baby to feed on its mother's milk for a long time) and **abstinence** (choosing not to have sexual relations).

Some modern methods of contraception use devices to prevent **fertilization**—the union of a male's sperm cell with a female's egg cell. Without fertilization, pregnancy cannot occur. These devices include **condoms,** which men wear, and **IUDs** and **diaphragms,** which are put inside a woman's body. Drugs, such as **birth-control pills,** also can keep a woman from getting pregnant. In general, these pills are taken daily.

For centuries, women have used long-term breastfeeding—perhaps for a year or two—as a way to reduce the chances of pregnancy. This method of birth control delays a woman's body from making the eggs that produce babies. Prolonged breastfeeding does not always work to prevent pregnancy.

CHINA'S ONE-CHILD PROGRAM

Li Fang is eight years old and lives with his parents in a village in eastern China. Li Fang's country has more than one billion inhabitants —one-fifth of the world's entire population. About one-fourth of China's people are under the age of 15. To keep the number from growing even larger, the government encourages couples to have only one child.

Although Li Fang has no brothers or sisters, he is not lonely. He and his parents live in a set of dwellings that also houses his aunts, uncles, cousins, and grandparents. They share chores, the vegetables from their garden, and livestock. They also eat together.

China launched its program to limit family size in the 1970s. At that time, the country realized that providing food, health care, and education for one billion people was costing too much money. Husbands and wives participate in family planning, which is achieved mainly through modern birth-control methods.

Having more than one child is not against the law, but the government rewards couples who follow the program. For example, people who have one child are first on lists for

A billboard in China promotes the idea of couples having only one child.

new housing. They also receive additional money per month, and their child gets a free education. These benefits are not as available to families with more than one child.

INDIA'S GROWING PAINS

India, a country in southern Asia, has a high birth rate, a high death rate among infants, and a large population. Estimates suggest that India's population of 859 million will top one billion by the year 2010.

This situation will affect Vimla Bhatt very seriously. She and her family try to live off a small piece of land in northern India. Because Vimla is a girl, she is already at a disadvantage in her culture, which values boys more highly than girls. Most families with only female children continue to have babies until boys are born. When money becomes scarce, parents usually give sons—rather than daughters—the advantages of schooling.

The Indian government has long recognized that rapid population growth is the nation's biggest problem. In fact, leaders want India to achieve *zero* population growth by 2050. Toward this effort, the government has made laws that grant women more rights in India's male-dominated society. To promote small families, the government also gives money to couples who have only one or two children. As a result of these changes, Vimla's choices about her family's size will probably be very different from the choices her mother had.

A health-care worker shares information about birth control with a group of Indian women.

At a rural clinic in Ghana, West Africa, a nurse gives advice and family-planning supplies to a woman from a nearby village.

Abortion is a method of ending an unwanted pregnancy. Human beings have long practiced abortion, which removes a **fetus**—an unborn, developing human being—from a woman's body. In ancient times, this removal was accomplished by drinking herbal mixtures, chemicals, or other substances that made a woman's body reject the fetus. In the modern era, doctors usually remove the fetus through surgery.

For some people, abortion is not an acceptable form of birth control. Since the mid-1800s, many nations have made laws—for medical or religious reasons—that limit the availability of abortion.

A DIFFERENT PROBLEM IN HUNGARY

Ten-year-old Miklos Hoos is the middle child in his family, which lives in Budapest, the capital of Hungary. He has an 18-year-old brother, and his mother recently gave birth to a baby girl. Years ago, the government of Hungary wanted people to limit the number of children they had. Now the government worries that there will be too many old people and encourages more births.

Hungary, which lies in eastern Europe, has a population of 10 million. One-fifth of the nation's population is under the age of 15, and one-seventh is older than 65. In recent years, the country has recorded more deaths than births. Thus, the number of Hungarians is decreasing, and older people make up a larger part of the population.

Hungary's low birth rate has advantages. With fewer people, the country has more jobs, food, and educational opportunities to share. But officials think the cost of caring for so many elderly Hungarians will be too high. They want the birth rate to rise so that there will be more young, working Hungarians—like Miklos and his brother and sister—to pay for future services to retired citizens.

The customers at a flower stall in Budapest, Hungary, reflect the growing number of older people in the country.

Sterilization, a medical operation, provides permanent birth control. It can be performed on a woman or a man. The procedure cuts the tubes through which a woman's egg or a man's sperm must travel for pregnancy to happen.

THE CHALLENGES AHEAD

Many challenges remain in the areas of contraception and family planning. We have to educate people all over the world about the benefits of small families. We also need to ease the conditions that encourage couples to have large families. For example, people might have fewer children if they had enough money to live and if they did not worry about providing for themselves as they grow older.

We must develop safer, more reliable, and simpler forms of contraception. A busy woman, for instance, may forget to take her birth-control pill each day. For this reason, sirens screech at 5 P.M. daily in Indonesia to remind women to take their birth-control pills.

We need to make methods of birth control easy for people everywhere to find and to use. In cultures that do not accept modern methods, natural birth-control techniques need to be researched and funded.

People sometimes have large families because they want to make sure someone will be there to take care of them when they are old.

CHAPTER SIX

LEARNING TO LIVE WITH LESS

❖ Question: When is 1 person really 10 people?

❖ Answer: When he or she has a high standard of living.

People who live in the developed nations of the world use a huge share of the earth's resources. Their impact on the earth is at least *10 times* greater than the effect of people living in the Third World.

For example, the 1.2 billion people in developed countries drive most of the 500 million cars on our planet. These cars use one-third of the world's oil. They pour tons of CO_2 and other compounds into the air.

(Left) People in developed nations drive most of the cars that exist in the world. (Right) Since cars spew poisonous fumes into the air, many citizens —such as these commuters in Denmark—choose to ride bicycles to get around.

These pollutants cause global warming and acid rain, both of which affect everyone on earth.

WHAT CAN WE DO?

More and more people now see that citizens in the developed countries need to change how they live. Here are just a few ways each of us can put less strain on the earth's resources.

REDUCE GARBAGE. If we create less, we have less to throw away. The average U.S. family produces 100 pounds (45 kilograms) of trash a week. Much of this amount is paper and plastic used in packaging. We can reduce the packaging materials we throw away. For example, when you purchase something small, avoid taking it from the store in a bag.

REUSE, RECYCLE, DO WITHOUT. People in the United States throw out 432,000 tons (392,000 metric tons) of garbage every day. Much of this amount ends up in the sea or in landfills. By comparison, the Japanese recycle 95 percent of

The recycling of aluminum cans saves most of the energy and natural resources that are needed to make brand-new aluminum containers.

their newspapers, 66 percent of their bottles, and 40 percent of their aluminum.

AVOID STYROFOAM CONTAINERS. Manufactured from CFCs, goods made of plastic foam also release CFCs when they are burned. Ask your favorite fast-food chain to wrap your hamburger in paper rather than in Styrofoam. Let the

KIDS AGAINST POLLUTION

In 1987, fifth-graders at Tenakill School in Closter, New Jersey, formed Kids Against Pollution (KAP). The students use their combined influence to change policies in their school, school district, and state that harm the environment.

One of KAP's first targets was the plastic foam (Styrofoam) that the school district used in the cafeterias. Tenakill's students knew that the Styrofoam plates, cups, and containers in cafeterias and fast-food chains are made from chemicals that destroy the ozone layer. This thin shield protects our planet from the sun's harmful rays.

The students presented the facts about plastic foam to the Closter school board, and its members agreed to stop using such containers in the district's schools. Glowing with their success, KAP then pressured the city council to pass a law to limit the use of Styrofoam. After three years of public hearings and debates, that fight was also successful.

Members of Closter's KAP have brought their concerns to people at every level of government. As one student said to politi- cians in Washington, D.C., "This generation is charging against the environment on my credit card." There are now hundreds of KAP chapters around the United States and in several foreign countries. For further information about starting a chapter, you can contact *Kids Against Pollution; Tenakill School; 275 High Street; Closter, New Jersey 07624.*

"SAVE THE EARTH NOT JUST FOR US BUT FOR FUTURE GENERATIONS"

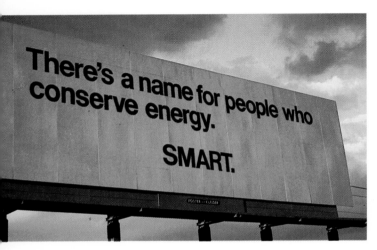

Conserving energy wherever we can lessens our impact on the earth's environment.

restaurant know why you are asking for a paper container.

■ *CONSERVE ENERGY.* Turn off lights, radios, and other users of electricity when you do not need them. U.S. citizens use a lot of electrical power, and the facilities that make our electricity cause pollution.

■ *USE WATER CAREFULLY.* Each person in the United States uses at least 80 gallons (303 liters) of water a day at home. Daily U.S. water consumption is

more than 70 times the amount that people in Ghana, West Africa, use. Many simple changes in our daily routines can reduce the amount of water we use. For instance, turn off the water while you are brushing your teeth, and be on the lookout for leaky faucets.

■ *USE OTHER TRANSPORTATION BESIDES CARS.* Our planet would have less pollution if there were fewer cars. Mass-transit systems—buses, subways, and

Water Used In An Average Day

	gallons	Liters
To brush our teeth twice a day with the water running.	4	15
To wash our hands with the water running.	2	8
To flush a toilet takes seven gallons. We do this at least three times a day.	21	79
To take a ten-minute shower.	50	189
To wash dishes in an automatic dishwasher.	12	45
	89	336

In doing just these few tasks, we've used 89 gallons (336 liters) of water in a single day !!

trains—are good alternatives to cars because they carry many people at once. And bicycles are the cleanest and cheapest form of transportation. Half of Denmark's 5.1 million people use bicycles to get around, and many Danish roads have special bike lanes.

PLANT TREES. Fully grown trees use up some of the CO_2 created by burning fossil fuels. In addition, trees decrease erosion. They are also natural coolants, providing a way to keep cool without fans, which use electricity, and without air conditioners, which contain CFCs.

A brother and sister read directions before planting tree seedlings. Trees produce oxygen—the gas we all need for breathing. These plants also absorb CO_2, which we make when we breathe out. Cars and factories create even more CO_2. Thus, trees have a hard time supplying our growing population with fresh oxygen.

CHAPTER SEVEN

HOW DO PEOPLE CHANGE?

In 1984, the United Nations held a World Population Conference in Mexico City. Many of the nations that attended signed the World Population Plan of Action. This list of proposals promotes concern for the earth's ecosystem. It stresses the need for money—from governments and from private citizens—to fund worldwide family-planning activities.

Studies show that about $20 would enable each couple in the developing world to practice family planning for a year. Many poor countries are struggling to

(Left) The many members of an extended family live together in Bangladesh—a southern Asian nation with 116 million people. This Third-World country supports family planning, even though funds for such services are limited. One-third of Bangladesh's married women use birth control.

supply basic necessities and cannot afford to fund family-planning services. Yet without a population plan, these countries will become even less able to provide food, shelter, and jobs for their citizens.

SLOWLY BUT SURELY

The major efforts to slow population growth have occurred in the last 30 years. In the 1970s, for example, the number of women using birth control in Mexico, Malaysia, and Thailand rose sharply when these women were given the chance to use family-planning methods. Demographers estimate that two-thirds of the couples in the developed world now practice family planning. In the Third World, one-fifth of the couples limit their family's size on purpose.

A family of villagers enjoys its main meal of the day. In some cultures, a man with many children is valued more than a man with a few children. This cultural tradition encourages couples to have a lot of babies.

To promote change, we must understand what keeps people from changing. A complex set of factors can affect an individual's decisions about having children. Some people do not change because their society disapproves of birth-control methods. Others resist change because of religious beliefs, lack of education, and the limited role of women in making family decisions.

Cultural factors can also affect decisions about a family's size. In some countries, for example, the number of children a man has influences his status in his community. A man with eight children is sometimes respected more than a man with one child. If a man with a large family runs his household well, the other men in his village may believe he could shoulder more responsibilities, perhaps for the entire community.

However, not even demographers can predict individual decisions about family planning. For example, the Roman Catholic Church bans the use of birth control among its followers. Yet population growth rates are declining in several countries with large numbers of Catholic citizens. These places include Italy, Austria, Mexico, and Brazil.

Although the Roman Catholic Church discourages most birth-control methods, about half of the Catholic women in Mexico still use them.

People who live in cities often change their habits more easily than people in rural areas. Studies in the 1970s showed that in Bangladesh, Pakistan, and Colombia, urban women were twice as likely to use birth control as rural women were. But even this trend has not always proved true. Rural women in other countries—Indonesia, South Korea, Thailand, and Panama, for example—were not far behind city women in the use of birth control.

THE VITAL KEY

Education is a key to change. People alter their habits when they learn that doing something differently will make their lives better. Birth rates are declining in countries with high standards of living because these nations also educate their citizens about the benefits of having small families.

In places where the level of education for women is going up, the use of family planning is also rising. When contraceptive use increases, birth rates decline. In countries that follow the Muslim

Women in Indonesia, a country in southeastern Asia, are better educated than their mothers were. Because female citizens can easily get information about family planning, Indonesia's birth rate has dropped sharply in the last 20 years.

religion—such as Bangladesh, Pakistan, and some Arab states—most women are not well educated. Nor do they have much power in making important family deci-

sions. These countries usually have high birth rates.

Java—a large island in Indonesia—is part of the Muslim world. It is also one of the world's most densely populated pieces of land. The Indonesian government strongly supports schooling on Java. Armed with their education, Javanese women are better equipped to make decisions about their work and their families. Java's birth rate is falling, because women are choosing to have fewer children.

WORKING TOGETHER

Many human activities harm the earth's environment, including the high standards of living in developed nations and the high growth rates in developing countries. To safeguard our planet's ecosystem and resources, changes will have to take place among people in both the developed and the developing world.

Until people learn a better way, they will continue to live as they always have. The things we already know are easy. Unknown

LIFE IN THE LAND OF PLENTY

Tess Mahoney has just turned two years old, and her parents and family have gathered to watch her tear into her presents. She received many toys, some that are just for fun and others that help her to learn about shapes and letters.

The Mahoney family lives in St. Paul, the capital of Minnesota, a state in the central United States. U.S. birth rates are low, but the use of the earth's resources—such as fuel, fresh water, and land—is high.

Because Tess's mother wanted to keep a high-paying job as a computer expert, she waited until she was 35 to have a child. Tess's father agreed with this plan, since it would give the family a larger income. With two incomes, the Mahoneys were able to buy a roomy house with a big backyard. They could afford two cars. By the time Tess came along, her parents had achieved a high standard of living.

To make sure that they have enough money to support how they live, Mrs. Mahoney returned to work soon after Tess was born. The Mahoneys do not plan to have any other children. They hope that their decision will make it possible for them to give their daughter a good life.

Most people in the developed world have a high standard of living that allows them to buy many goods.

Cultures in the developed and the developing world add to our population problems in different ways. A Kenyan family's numbers (left) are one side of the issue. A U.S. family's use of fuel and other resources (right) make up the flip side of the population coin.

things are hard to imagine and sometimes even a little scary.

For example, people who live in developed countries drive cars because they provide a quick and easy way to travel. We are so used to driving cars that we may not be able to imagine any other way of getting around. Yet more people are telling us that the use of 500 million cars is bad for the environment.

If you met a family from Kenya with eight children, you might be tempted to say, "You have so many children! Don't you know better?" The mother or father from Kenya might turn to you and say, "Your family has two cars! Don't *you* know better?" Cultures must be patient with one another. Cultures must learn from one another. Learning from one another is the key to change.

ORGANIZATIONS

THE BASIC FOUNDATION
P. O. Box 47012
St. Petersburg, Florida 33743

**PLANNED PARENTHOOD
FEDERATION OF AMERICA**
810 Seventh Avenue
New York, New York 10019

POPULATION CRISIS COMMITTEE
1120 19th Street NW, Suite 550
Washington, D.C. 20036

POPULATION INSTITUTE
110 Maryland Avenue NE, Suite 207
Washington, D.C. 20002

POPULATION REFERENCE BUREAU
1875 Connecticut Avenue NW, Suite 520
Washington, D.C. 20009

**UNITED NATIONS FUND
ON POPULATION ACTIVITIES**
220 East 42nd Street
New York, New York 10017

WORLDWATCH INSTITUTE
1776 Massachusetts Avenue NW
Washington, D.C. 20036

ZERO POPULATION GROWTH
1400 16th Street NW, Suite 320
Washington, D.C. 20036

Photo Acknowledgments

Photographs are used courtesy of: p. 4, NASA; pp. 6, 60, 62, American Lutheran Church; p. 7, Royal Embassy of Saudi Arabia; pp. 12, 32, 61, Inter-American Development Bank; p. 13 (left), Center for Afghanistan Studies; p. 13 (right), Josh Kohnstamm; p. 14, Tourisme Côte d'Ivoire; p. 15, Sandi and Jim Provencher; p. 16, Ken Kragen/USA for Africa; p. 17, Australian Tourism Commission; pp. 20, 25, Library of Congress; p. 21 (left), UPI/Bettmann; p. 21 (right), Royal Norwegian Embassy; p. 22, Steve Brosnahan; p. 23, Mobil Oil Corporation; p. 24, Earl H. Lubensky; p. 26 (left), National Association of Conservation Districts; pp. 26 (right), 42, UNICEF; p. 27, Herbert Fristedt; p. 28, NASA/Goddard Space Flight Center; p. 30, Florida Department of Commerce; p. 31, Sierra Club of Ontario; p. 33, Ch. Errath/FAO; p. 34 (left), Patty Leslie/Center for Plant Conservation; p. 34 (right), Richard R. Hewett; p. 35, Center for Environmental Education; p. 36, Tom O'Toole; p. 37, Leonard Soroka; p. 38, Kay Shaw Photography; p. 39 (top), Jim Cron; p. 39 (bottom), David Mangurian; p. 40, Kerstin Coyle; p. 41, Steve Feinstein; p. 43, F. Botts/FAO; p. 44, Nigel Harvey; p. 45, Dr. Deborah Pellow; p. 46, Minnesota Department of Transportation; p. 47, © Blaine Harrington III; p. 48, Wisconsin Department of Natural Resources; p. 50, David Falconer; p. 51, Bill Rooney; p. 52, World Bank; p. 54, J. Van Acker/FAO; p. 55, Tom Moran; p. 56, Mary Gunderson; p. 57, Jay A. Beck; p. 58 (left), Phil Porter; p. 58 (right), Colleen Sexton. Charts and illustrations by: pp. 8–9, 10–11, Laura Westlund; pp. 18, 50, Bryan Liedahl.

Front Cover: J. G. Fuller/The Hutchison Library
Back Cover: (left) Kay Chernush/Agency for International Development; (right) Mobil Oil Corporation

abortion: the removal of a fetus from a woman's body before the fetus can survive on its own.

abstinence (AB-sti-nints): a decision to prevent pregnancy by not engaging in sexual relations.

antibiotic (ant-i-by-OT-ik): a drug given by doctors that can kill or stop the growth of disease-carrying bacteria.

bacteria (bak-TEER-i-yah): groups of very small organisms (micro-organisms) that can cause disease.

birth control: regulating the number of children born, especially by preventing pregnancy.

Cutting wood to burn as fuel can lead to desertification in countries with few forests.

birth-control pill: a drug taken by a woman that causes her body to stop producing eggs.

birth rate: the number of live births each year for every 1,000 people in a nation's population.

carbon dioxide: a gas that is naturally found in the air and that combines with water to form carbonic acid.

chloro-fluoro-carbons (CFCs): chemicals made up of chlorine, fluorine, and carbon that have many industrial uses. CFCs are part of the manufacture of plastic foam (Styrofoam) that we use for packaging and in containers.

condom: a soft plastic sheath that traps a man's sperm.

contraception (kon-tra-SEP-shun): the process of using methods, devices, or drugs to keep a male's sperm from fertilizing a female's egg.

death rate: the number of deaths each year for every 1,000 people in a nation's population.

deforestation: the large-scale cutting and burning of trees.

desertification: making deserts through deforestation and overgrazing.

developed (industrialized) nations: countries that have a high standard of living because they have developed their natural resources and have a wide variety of finished products to sell.

developing (Third-World) nations: countries that have a low standard of living because they are just beginning to develop their natural resources and have few industries.

diaphragm (DIE-uh-fram): a plastic cap put inside a woman's body to prevent fertilization.

ecosystem: a complex community of living and nonliving things that exists as a balanced unit in nature.

epidemic: an outbreak of a disease that spreads easily and that affects many people at the same time.

erosion (ih-RO-zhun): the wearing or washing away of soil by water or wind.

exhaustible: able to be used up completely.

extinct: no longer existing.

famine (FAM-en): a severe shortage of food that causes starvation in a wide area.

El Salvador, a crowded country in Central America, is one of the world's developing nations.

fertilizer: a natural or chemical substance added to the soil to help plants grow.

fertilization: the union of a man's sperm cell with a woman's egg cell.

fetus (FEET-is): an unborn, developing human being.

finite (FY-night): having a limit.

fossil fuels: substances, such as coal and petroleum, that slowly developed from the remains of living things.

immunization: the process of protecting people from a disease by injecting them with a small dose of its germs so the human body can develop an immunity (resistance) to the sickness.

infant mortality: deaths occurring in the first year of life.

Flame trees, characterized by their fiery red blossoms, are a species of tropical plant.

influenza: an easily spread disease that affects the human breathing system and that is characterized by sudden fever and aches, weakness of the body, and chills.

IUD: a small device put inside a woman's body that prevents her egg from being fertilized.

life expectancy: the expected length of someone's life based on statistics.

pesticide (PES-ti-side): a chemical used to destroy insects or other pests.

population growth rate: the speed with which a population increases over time.

prolonged breastfeeding: allowing a baby to feed on its mother's milk for a long time as a way to reduce the chances of pregnancy.

species (SPEE-sheez): a kind of living thing.

standard of living: how rich a nation's citizens are, measured by access to necessities and luxuries.

sterilization: the process of making someone unable to produce children.

topsoil: the surface layer of dirt in which plants grow.

tropics: the hot, wet region that forms a broad belt around the middle of the earth.

zero population growth (ZPG): a balance between the birth rate and the death rate that keeps the population from increasing.

INDEX